UPCYCLE!

TURN EVERYDAY OBJECTS INTO HOME DECOR

P9-CRH-309

Sonia Lucano

Photography by Frédéric Lucano

UPCYCLE!

TURN EVERYDAY OBJECTS INTO HOME DECOR

50 EASY DIY PROJECTS

weldon**owen**

CONTENTS

PREFACE

While recycling today is trendy, I want to take it even further . . . not by decorating our homes with second-hand objects, but by starting with everyday objects that we have at home or can find easily.

I propose that you "upcycle" or repurpose these objects, so common and ordinary that we lose sight of their decorative potential: crates, wood pallets, white cotton sheets, glass jars, wine bottles, tin cans, white dishes, lampshades, and more.

Here are fifty ideas for easily transforming these objects into budget-friendly design creations that will add a "rustic chic" flair to any home's decor. No need to be an expert in do-it-yourself crafts. All that's needed is the desire to implement the projects in this book.

PALLETS

In some cities, it's common to see pallets free for the taking in an industrial warehouse district, behind big-box stores, or at building sites. They can be new and unfinished or old and weathered. They come in a wide variety: solid or with slats spaced at wider intervals, light or heavy . . . You can chose something specific or leave it to chance, depending on the project you have in mind. Alternatively, you can buy them new—search the Internet for a vendor in your area as deliveries can be expensive.

STENCILED SHELF

Decorate an unfinished-wood curio shelf with a gracefully-painted word or phrase.

TOOLS

crowbar
hammer
pliers
screwdriver
jigsaw
sander (or
medium- and
fine-grade
sandpaper)
drill
fine-tipped
brush
number 2 pencil

SUPPLIES

1 pallet
4 1½-inch
screws
tracing and
carbon papers
black wood
paint

INSTRUCTIONS

• **Choose a pallet** with weathered wood. Saw off a section of the pallet as indicated below to make the main part of the shelf [fig. 1].

• **Remove one slat from the bottom** of the pallet. Start by lifting the slat and carefully prying it up with the crowbar at the connection point. Repeat for each point that's nailed down. Turn the removed slat over, and loosen the nails by tapping on their points with the hammer. Turn the slat back over, and finish removing the nails with the pliers.

• **Place this slat under the sawed-off segment** to form the shelf's bottom. Drive one screw into each corner [fig. 2].

• **Use an electric sander** (or medium-grade sandpaper) to get rid of splinters. Finish with fine sandpaper to make the wood nice and smooth.

• **Drill 2 holes** 1 3/16 inch from the top at each end [fig. 3]. You'll use these holes to hang the shelf on the wall. Alternatively, you can attach metal hangers to the back of the shelf.

• **Decorate as you wish. Here, I traced the phrase** from page 138 and transfered it onto the wood using carbon paper. Then, I filled it in using a fine-tipped brush.

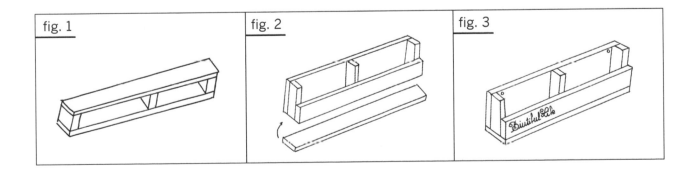

| fig. 1 | fig. 2 | fig. 3 |

FLOOR LAMP

A funky, rustic floor lamp for ambient light.

TOOLS

hammer
pliers
screwdriver
jigsaw
sander (or medium- and fine-grade sandpaper)
drill
number 2 pencil
fine and medium brushes

SUPPLIES

1 pallet
porcelain light bulb socket with mounting bracket
light bulb
black lamp cord with switch and plug
tracing and carbon papers
white, matte wood paint

INSTRUCTIONS

• **Choose a pallet** with wood that's a bit weathered. Using the saw, segment the pallet as indicated below [fig. 1].

• **Use an electric sander** (or medium-grade sandpaper) to get rid of splinters. Finish with fine-grade sandpaper to make the wood nice and smooth.

• **Apply a light coat of paint** on the wood. Use a light touch to get a somewhat rough effect. Let dry completely.

• **To add an industrial feel, add a stencil; I used the number "61802"** from the pattern on page 139. You can use carbon paper to transfer it to the interior of the lamp. Then paint it using a fine-tipped brush.

• **Drill a hole** in the bottom for the electric cord to pass through [fig. 2]. Fasten the light bulb mounting bracket by screwing it in just above the hole.

• **Insert the electric cord** through the hole—leaving the plug and switch on the outside—and connect the cord to the socket. Mount the socket on the bracket with the little screw that came with it, and then screw in the light bulb.

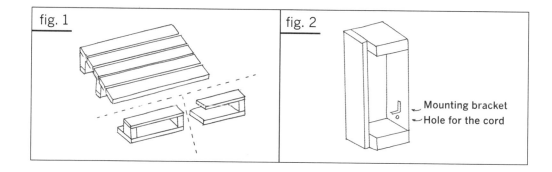

fig. 1

fig. 2

Mounting bracket
Hole for the cord

«STARS» HEADBOARD

To fill your head with dreams . . .

TOOLS

crowbar
hammer
pliers
electric
screwdriver
jigsaw
number 2
pencil
small roller
fine-tipped
brush

SUPPLIES

5 pallets
(19 slats
about 3 Inches
wide)
60 1 1/2-inch
screws
medium and fine
grade sandpaper
carbon paper
off-white matte
wood paint

INSTRUCTIONS

• **Choose pallets** with wood that's a bit weathered. Dismantle them completely in order to salvage the slats from the bottoms. Your headboard should be around 5 feet wide for a bed that's 4 1/2 feet wide. You will need about 19 slats for the headboard, depending on the pallet. Dismantle the pallet, going slowly so as not to split the wood. Begin by lifting each slat and carefully prying it up with the crowbar at the connection point. Repeat for all the points where there are nails. Turn the removed slats over and loosen the nails by tapping on their points with the hammer. Turn them back over and finish removing the nails with the pliers. Line up the slats next to each other on the ground, right side down [fig. 1].

• **Remove six more slats** from the bottoms of the pallets for your "support" slats. Lay the slats perpendicularly on the lined-up slats: two across the top (end-to-end), two across the middle, and two across the bottom [fig 1].

• **Screw the support slats** to the headboard slats. Turn the headboard over so it's right side up.

• **Use medium-grade sandpaper** to get rid of any splinters. Finish off with fine-grade sandpaper in order to lightly smooth the wood.

• **Draw a light line** about 8 inches down from the top. Apply the off-white paint unevenly below this line. Intentionally leave irregular roller marks.

• **Trace the word "STARS"** on page 140, and transfer it using the carbon paper onto the unpainted wood section on top. Then fill it in using the fine brush.

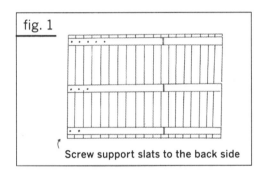

fig. 1

Screw support slats to the back side

BLACK COFFEE TABLE

Paint a pallet black for an elegant coffee table . . . with an upcycled twist!

TOOLS

crowbar
hammer
pliers
screwdriver
saw or jigsaw
medium brush
medium roller

SUPPLIES

1 pallet
40 x 48 inches
(with no loose
slats)
1 pallet for
salvaging four
wood cubes
3 2-inch screws
medium-grade
sandpaper
black wood
paint
wood glue

INSTRUCTIONS

• **Saw the pallet** as indicated in the drawing, to shorten it from 48 inches to 32 inches This way you will have a 40 x 32-inch table [fig.1].

• **Salvage the slat from the bottom** part that won't be visible. Begin by lifting the slat with the crowbar, and carefully prying at the connection point. Repeat for all the points where there are nails. Turn the removed slat over, and loosen the nails by tapping on their points with the hammer. Turn the slat back over, and finish removing the nails with the pliers.

• **Lay the removed slat underneath**, on the bottom edge of the length, where you just sawed. Attach it to the end by driving in the screws. You have now created a handy shelf below your table [fig. 2].

• **Roughly sand the entire table** in order to get rid of splinters, but make sure that you keep some of the interesting texture.

• **Paint the entire table black.** Apply two coats, two hours apart (refer to the directions on the paint can).

• **Remove the wood cubes** from the second pallet using the crowbar again. Work carefully, little by little, in order to avoid splitting the cubes.

• **Paint the four cubes black**, in two coats. Allow them to dry completely, and then glue them to the four corners of the table with wood glue.

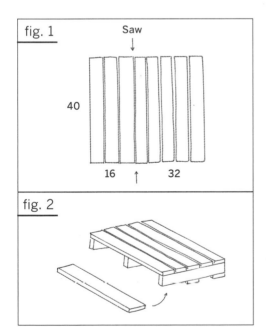

fig. 1

Saw

40

16   32

fig. 2

MINI-SHELF

Ideal in a hallway . . . for little treasures and tiny plants.

TOOLS

crowbar
hammer
pliers
screwdriver
small roller
medium round
sash brush

SUPPLIES

2 40 x 32-inch pallets
12 medium screws
4 small (1 3/16-inch) metal brackets
medium grade sandpaper
pale matte gray wood paint

INSTRUCTIONS

• **Keep one pallet intact,** and take apart the second one in order to salvage three nice slats that will serve as the shelves. Begin by lifting the slat with the crowbar and carefully forcing it apart at the connection point. Repeat for all the points where there are nails. Turn the removed slat over and loosen the nails by tapping on their points with the hammer. Turn the slat back over and finish removing the nails with the pliers.

• **Stand the pallet vertically** so that the slats are horizontal. Place the first unattached slat on top of the pallet, and fasten it with two screws at each end [fig. 1].

• **Now install the other two loose slats** over the existing slats of the pallet. Place one at the top third of the pallet, and the other one a bit lower.

• **Keep these slats in place** by attaching a small bracket to each end of the slat; one end of the bracket is screwed into the bottom of the added slat, the other into the existing pallet.

• **Sand roughly with medium-grade sandpaper** all over to get rid of splinters.

• **Roughly apply the pale-gray paint** using the roller, and allow it to dry. Use the round sash brush to fill in gaps and small spaces.

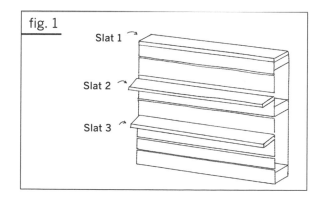

fig. 1

Slat 1
Slat 2
Slat 3

MESSAGE BOARD

Remind yourself what's important in life.

TOOLS

saw
number 2 pencil
fine brush

SUPPLIES

3 pallet slats
carbon paper
black wood
paint

INSTRUCTIONS

• **Saw the slats up** to make five small boards, each of them 16 inches long.

• **Next, stencil inspirational words** or phrases onto them. Choose your own or trace the ones I've provided on pages 141 to 143. Transfer them onto the slats using carbon paper, then paint them using the fine brush.

• **Hang the boards on the wall,** to help inspire creativity and positivity.

STRAPPED SIDE TABLE

Assemble like a building-block set to make a solid wood table!

TOOLS

crowbar
hammer
pliers
jigsaw

SUPPLIES

2 pallets
longs nails
medium-grade
sandpaper
2 canvas
luggage straps

INSTRUCTIONS

• **Take the pallets apart:** begin by lifting each slat with the crowbar and carefully prying it off at the connection point. Repeat for all the points where there are nails, and then for all the slats. Turn the removed slats over and loosen the nails by tapping on their points with the hammer. Turn them back over, and finish removing the nails with the pliers. You'll need 36 slats for a roughly 9 x 9-inch table.

• **Using the jigsaw, cut all the slats** all to the same length, around 17 or 18 inches.

• **Lay three slats on top** of each other, and nail them together. This creates a long, solid block, which will make it easier to assemble the rest. Continue this process to make a total of nine blocks of three slats each. Stand the blocks upright, and add one loose slat to each block, to hide the nails for the table's exterior.

• **Turn each block** so that it's perpendicular to its neighbor, and form a 3-by-3-block square [see photograph]. Hold them together with the two straps; tighten one on top and the other below.

• **Sand roughly with medium-grade sandpaper** all over to get rid of splinters.

PERSONALIZED WALL HANGERS

Every member of the household gets their own personalized hanger.

TOOLS

crowbar
hammer
pliers
jigsaw
drill
large brush

SUPPLIES

1 pallet
medium grade
sandpaper
2 ½-inch
copper nails (2
for each hanger)
alphabet stamps
black ink
wood paint in
various colors

INSTRUCTIONS

• **Using your saw, cut up the pallet as indicated** below to obtain a block made up of the cube and part of the slat [fig. 1]. Continue to make as many pieces as you like for your hangers. [fig. 1] .

• **Use medium-grade sandpaper** to roughly sand away any splinters, but don't sand it too much because you want to keep some of the interesting texture.

• **Make a small hole** with the drill in the center, about 1 inch from the top, so that you can hang it on the wall.

• **Paint the blocks and the slats** in assorted colors that go with your decor.

• **Place two nails in each block about** an inch from the top, to serve as coat hangers.

• **Stamp each person's name** on their hanger, centering it, about 4 inches below the top of the hanger [fig. 2].

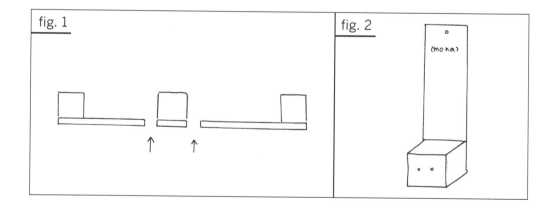

fig. 1

fig. 2

NUMBER CUBES

A funky decor item or a way to teach your kids about numbers.

TOOLS

crowbar
hammer
pliers
round sash
brush
very fine-tipped
brush
number 2 pencil

SUPPLIES

3 pallets
medium- and
fine-grade
sandpaper
very-light gray
wood paint
2-inch-wide
masking tape
tracing and
carbon papers
black wood
paint

INSTRUCTIONS

• **Salvage 10 wood cubes** from the pallets: begin by lifting the slat with the crowbar, and carefully forcing it apart at each connection point. Repeat for all the slats at all points where there are nails. In this way, remove all the slats and cubes.

• **Sand the cubes.** If you're intending to let a child play with them, use medium-grade sandpaper, followed by fine-, to eliminate all possible splinters. If you'll be using them for decoration, leave them rough.

• **Use the masking tape to block areas** of the cubes not to be painted, as in the drawing [fig. 1]. Vary the shapes by masking different parts of the cubes with different widths.

• **Use the round sash brush to paint the cubes light gray**, somewhat roughly. Let dry completely.

• **Trace the numbers** on page 139 and transfer them onto the cubes using carbon paper and pencil. Then paint the numbers in with a very fine-tipped brush.

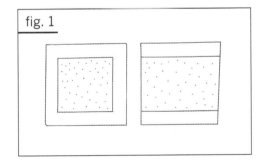

fig. 1

CANDLESTICK CUBES

Use unfinished wood cubes to make rustic, chic candlesticks.

TOOLS

crowbar
drill
auger bit, 1-inch
diameter
clamp

SUPPLIES

wood cubes
from a pallet

INSTRUCTIONS

• **Salvage the wood cubes** from the pallets. Begin by lifting the slat with the crowbar and carefully prying it up at each connection point. Repeat for all the slats at every point that's nailed down. Remove all the slats and cubes in this way. If you want to make the cubes more interesting, look for those that have something printed on them. You can also burn, paint, or stamp whatever you like on your cubes as well.

• **Put the auger bit in your drill;** clamp the cube firmly (or have someone hold it for you carefully) and begin to drill slowly, being sure to keep the drill exactly vertical.

• **Make the hole about an inch deep.** It's not necessary for the hole to be perfectly in the center of the cube. Insert a candle, and light it!

WOOD CRATES

While you may be able to get lucky and find some unwanted crates at farmer's markets or some supermarkets, wooden crates are readily available at most craft stores; you can find them in a range of sizes depending on what they were intended to hold. They're unfinished, so they're ready to be painted. For larger crates, you can look for pretty, older ones with weathered wood and lettering; these are usually wine or apple crates. To find nice ones, look around flea markets, garage sales, eBay, or Craigslist. IKEA also has plain, unfinished pine crates.

FIRE-LOG HOLDER

A rolling crate is an attractive way to hold logs.

TOOLS

utility knife
medium, round
sash brush
fine-tipped
brush
number 2 pencil
screwdriver

SUPPLIES

1 apple or wine
bottle crate
2-inch wide
masking tape
off-white, matte
wood paint
tracing and
carbon papers
4 casters, 1 $3/16$-
inch diameter
16 little screws

INSTRUCTIONS

• **Clean the crate well with soap and water** and dry completely. Use the utility knife to cut the masking tape into strips, and place the strips diagonally on the front of the crate about 4 inches apart.

• **Paint the stripes** off-white; let dry, and apply a second coat. Let dry.

• **Use the "fire" stencil** on page 140 to trace the word, and then transfer it to the top slat using the carbon paper and pencil. Paint the letters in off-white with the fine brush.

• **Turn the crate upside-down,** and attach the casters to the corners using the screwdriver.

FIRE

LOUNGING BENCH

Simply turn over wine crates and sew a little cushion to make a pretty bench.

TOOLS

sewing machine
fabric scissors
needle
number 2 pencil
clothes iron

SUPPLIES

2 wood crates
1 twin-size white cotton sheet
quilt batting 80 x 40-inch
white thread
11 mother of pearl buttons, $^{11}/_{16}$-inch diameter

INSTRUCTIONS

- **Wash your sheet**, then lightly iron it (leaving it slightly wrinkled).

- **Cut two 42 x 14-inch rectangles** from your cotton bed sheet. Next, cut another strip that is 9 ft x 2 inches (i.e., the length of the sheet).

- **Sew the two long sides** of the strip together. Next, place this strip against the first rectangle, wrong sides together, and sew them together, leaving a $^3/_8$-inch hem. Place the second rectangle edge-to-edge with the length of the long strip. Sew them together, leaving a 7 $^1/_8$-inch opening.

- **Cut two 41 x 12 $^5/_8$-inch rectangles** of the quilt batting. Place one on top of the other, and insert them into the seat cushion through the opening. Position the batting so that it's nice and flat inside.

- **Fold the top opening $^3/_8$ inches over itself,** and sew it shut by hand.

- **Mark small dots with the pencil**, following the placement in the drawing, and sew on the 11 buttons, taking care to pass the needle vertically through all layers of cloth [fig. 1].

- **Lay the finished cushion** on the upside-down crates.

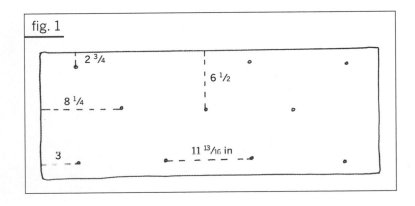

fig. 1

BOUND-UP BOOKCASE

Turn empty crates into a perfect, stylish bookcase for your space.

TOOLS

medium, round
sash brush
small roller
drill
fine drill bit
large pliers
or clamp
ruler
number 2 pencil

SUPPLIES

7 apple crates
white matte
wood paint
11-foot natural
leather strip,
3/16-inch wide

INSTRUCTIONS

• **Browse around for your crates.** They can be old and don't have to be identical. You can also get plain, untreated pine ones at IKEA or other home stores.

• **Paint the crates white**, somewhat roughly. Allow them to dry. Position them following the suggestion in the drawing [fig. 1].

• **Use a pencil to mark small dots** 2 inches from the edges of the crates at points where the crates will be connected, as in the drawing.

• **Start at the bottom.** Hold two crates together with the clamp (or pliers), and drill the crates at the same time. Make all the holes this way, repositioning the clamp and then drilling.

• **Cut the leather strip** into sixteen pieces, each 7 3/4 inches long. Pass them through the holes in order to tie the crates together. Knot them as in the drawing, nice and tight, to stabilize the bookcase [fig. 2].

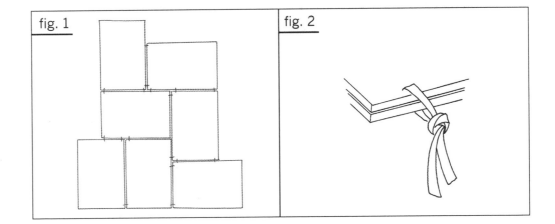

fig. 1

fig. 2

DECORATIVE CRATES

Hang crates on the wall and create small treasure boxes.

TOOLS

medium, round sash brush
very fine-tipped brush
number 2 pencil

SUPPLIES

crates of various sizes
dusty-rose, matte wood paint
tracing and carbon papers
black paint

INSTRUCTIONS

• **Choose a variety of crates.** Clementines and strawberries usually come in small wooden boxes that are perfect for this project; you can find larger ones at some farmer's markets, thrift stores, or craft stores.

• **Paint the crates entirely in dusty rose**, let them dry, and then apply a second coat.

• **Wait until the paint has completely dried, and then stencil the crates with words of your choice.** Here, I traced the words on page 144, and transfered them to the inside of the crates using carbon paper and pencil. Fill in the letters using the black paint and a very fine-tipped brush.

rose

HERB PLANTER

Grow some herbs or succulents indoors in an old crate.

TOOLS

staple gun

SUPPLIES

old wood crate
plastic sheeting
potting soil
variety of plants

INSTRUCTIONS

• **Choose a wood crate**; you can find them at yard sales, thrift stores, eBay, or on Craigslist.

• **Cover the interior of the crate** with plastic sheeting, stopping about an inch from the top. Then staple it to hold it in place.

• **Fill the crate with potting soil,** and plant your plants, flowers, succulents, or aromatic herbs. Don't hesitate to use plants of different heights. Water regularly, but moderately.

COTTON SHEETS

For these sheets, what's most important is that they're white and cotton. You can find old ones at thrift stores, eBay, or on Craigslist. They're best if they're fairly heavy and good-quality cotton. You can also use new sheets, of course.

ROUND POLKA-DOT TABLECLOTH

Beautify a table by draping it with a charming polka-dotted table cloth.

TOOLS

clothes iron
fabric scissors
needle
craft knife
number 2 pencil

SUPPLIES

1 twin-size
cotton sheet
cotton
embroidery
thread
fabric paint
1 potato
rag
twine
1 large nail

INSTRUCTIONS

• **Wash your sheet** even if it's new, then iron it (this gives the sheet a nice, slightly crinkly texture).

• **To cut the sheet in a circle,** you'll need a second person to help you. Begin by laying the sheet on the floor, nice and flat. Mark the center with the pencil. Use a string that is half the sheet's width plus 4 inches (for example, if your sheet is 70 inches wide, your string should be 39 inches long). Tie the pencil to one end and the nail to the other. One person kneels on the sheet, holding the nail at its center. The other draws a circle around the center, making sure that the string stays taut throughout. Then, carefully cut out the circle.

• **Cut 16 x 16-inch squares** to make napkins from the rest of the sheet.

• **To hem your tablecloth,** cut a piece of embroidery thread to about 24 inches. Separate the strands, and use only a single strand to thread your needle. Fold the edge of the fabric, and hem it using a blanket stitch (see page 149). Continue like this all the way around the tablecloth, folding and sewing as you go. Then do the same to hem your matching table napkins.

• **Make your stamp** by cutting a potato in half. Wipe off the cut side, and draw a circle in the center. Cut the potato away carefully, making a round stamp.

• **Spread some fabric paint on a plate** and dip your homemade stamp into it. Try it out on a piece of paper before starting on the tablecloth [fig. 1]! If you're happy with the result, stamp the dots, staying mostly near the edge of the tablecloth. Stamp some onto the napkins as well. Let dry completely.

• **Iron in order to set the paint;** be sure to follow the manufacturer's instructions.

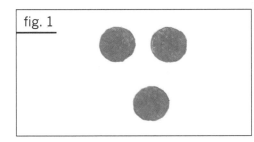

fig. 1

EMBROIDERED DAILY DISH TOWELS

Add a touch of the French countryside with these embroidered dish towels.

TOOLS

clothes iron
sewing machine
fabric scissors
number 2 pencil
needle

SUPPLIES

1 twin-size
cotton sheet
tracing and
carbon papers
1 skein of
black cotton
embroidery
thread
embroidery
needle

INSTRUCTIONS

• **Wash your sheet**, even if it's new, and then lightly iron it (leave it slightly wrinkled).

• **For each towel, cut an 18 $^1/_2$ x 24 $^1/_2$-inch rectangle.** This size includes enough for $^5/_8$-inch hems. Cut another 1 x 2 $^3/_4$-inch strip. Zigzag stitch the edges to prevent frays.

• **Sew a hem** all the way around the towel. Use the iron to fold it over twice: the first fold $^3/_{16}$ inch, the second $^3/_8$ inch. Stitch $^1/_4$ inch from the edges.

• **Next, fold the small strip** of sheet with the iron, as in the drawing and stitch $^1/_{16}$ inch from the edge [fig. 1]. Fold it in two to make a loop, and sew it to the top of the towel, at about a third of the width.

• **Embroider your towels.** Trace each day of the week (see pages 145–146), and transfer them to the towel using the carbon paper, 2 inches from the top of the left edge. Cut the embroidery thread to 24 inches, and separate out a single strand to use. Embroider the day of the week using a chain stitch (see page 149).

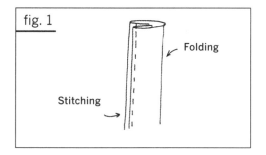

fig. 1

Folding

Stitching

BOLD TABLE RUNNERS

Idael for a minimalist table, a simple message painted in black on white.

TOOLS

clothes iron
fine-tipped
brush
fabric scissors
number 2 pencil

SUPPLIES

1 twin-size white
cotton sheet
black fabric
paint
carbon paper

INSTRUCTIONS

• **Wash your sheet** even if it's new, and then iron it.

• **Cut three 40 x 17 $^3/_4$-inch rectangles.**

• **Fold the hems using the iron.** First, fold over $^3/_{16}$ inch, then again $^3/_8$ inch, all the way around the rectangle, except for any edges with the sheet's original hem; in fact, the top edge of sheets often has nice, neat hems that can be pretty to use.

• **Trace the patterns** *"EAT," "GOOD,"* and *"FOOD"* (found on pages 147 and 148), and transfer each to the center of one of the rectangles using carbon paper and pencil.

• **Paint in the letters** with black paint and a fine-tipped brush. Let dry completely, then iron to set the paint, following the manufacturer's instructions.

GOOD

DIP-DYED CURTAIN

Soft natural shades, like olive, transform a white sheet into an eye-catching curtain.

TOOLS

washing
machine
large tub

SUPPLIES

1 twin-size
cotton sheet

olive green
fabric dye

salt

INSTRUCTIONS

• **Wash your sheet, even if it's new,** and then take it out of the machine, and shake it a couple of times to loosen the creases from the spin cycle.

• **Prepare your dye** in a large tub; add hot water and salt as indicated by the manufacturer's instructions.

• **Spread out the sheet,** and then fold it in half lengthwise and then once again to make a manageable width for dunking; you can also attach a hanger to one end. Plunge about half of its length into the tub, and let it soak about five minutes. Raise the curtain about a foot, leaving the rest to soak for ten more minutes. Repeat four times, each time lifting it out about a foot [fig. 1].

• **Wash your sheet,** and hang it out to air-dry.

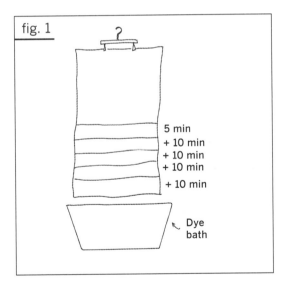

fig. 1

5 min
+ 10 min
+ 10 min
+ 10 min
+ 10 min

Dye
bath

SHEET-CHIC TOTE BAG

An everyday tote bag with natural leather handles.

TOOLS

iron
sewing machine
fabric scissors
needle
utility knife

SUPPLIES

1 twin size cotton sheet
1 yard natural leather strap, 1 $^3/_{16}$ inch wide
heavy-duty sewing thread

INSTRUCTIONS

• **Wash your sheet** even if it's new, then iron it lightly (leaving it slightly wrinkled).

• **Cut two 20 x 12 $^1/_2$-inch rectangles** (A). This size includes enough for $^3/_8$-inch hems. Then cut one 6 $^5/_{16}$ x 44-inch strip (B) and another 6 $^5/_{16}$ x 63 $^3/_4$ inches (C). Zigzag-stitch the edges of all the pieces to prevent fraying.

• **Lay the strip** (B) against one of the rectangles (A) right sides together, and sew $^3/_8$ inch from the edge of two widths and one of the lengths.

• **Lay the second rectangle** (A) edge-to-edge with the length of the other side of strip (B). Again, stitch the two widths and one length. Now take the band (C), and sew the two widths together. Lay the band (C) right side to right side of the sack on top [fig. 1].

• **Sew all the way around,** and turn the flap to the inside.

• **Cut the leather strap** in order to have two 18-inch handles, cutting the ends diagonally with the utility knife. Lay them on the outside of the sack 6 inches from the edge of each rectangle (A). Using a saddle stitch (see page 149), sew a $^3/_4$ x 1 $^3/_{16}$-inch rectangle.

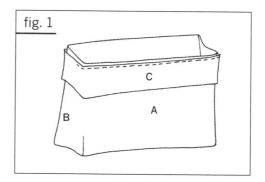

fig. 1

AN EMBROIDERED-CIRCLE PILLOW

A simple, whimsical pillow.

TOOLS

clothes iron
sewing machine
fabric scissors
needle
compass

SUPPLIES

1 twin-size
cotton sheet
1 bag of cotton
filling
white thread
cotton
embroidery
thread

INSTRUCTIONS

• **Wash your sheet** even if it's new, and then iron it lightly (leaving it slightly wrinkled).

• **Cut two 26 x 16 $^1/_2$-inch rectangles** out of the sheet. This includes a $^3/_8$-inch seam allowance. Zigzag-stitch the edges of the two pieces.

• **Using a compass**, draw an 11 $^3/_4$-inch circle in the center of one of the rectangles. Cut a 24-inch long piece of embroidery thread, and separate out a single strand to use. Embroider the circle using a chain stitch (see page 149).

• **Place the rectangles** right-side-together. Sew all the way around, leaving a 4 $^3/_4$-inch wide opening. Turn the pillow right-side out, and push out all the corners with your fingers.

• **Insert the filling**, then close the pillow by folding over $^3/_8$ inch on each side and hand-stitching it closed.

HANGING LAMP SHADE

This embroidered cotton shade gives you a nice, soft light.

TOOLS

clothes iron
sewing machine
fabric scissors
needle
compass
number 2 pencil

SUPPLIES

1 twin-size
cotton sheet
white thread
black cotton
embroidery
thread
1 cylindrical
hanging
lampshade
frame, 11 3/4-
inch diameter
(with a round
top and bottom)
double-sided
tape for
lampshades
1 black hanging-
lamp light cord
with socket
light bulb
tracing and
carbon papers

INSTRUCTIONS

• **Wash your sheet** even if it's new, then lightly iron it (leave it slightly wrinkled).

• **Cut a 38 x 13 $^3/_4$-inch rectangle**. This includes a $^3/_8$-inch seam allowance and a $^5/_8$-inch hem. Zigzag stitch the edges of the rectangle.

• **Trace the light-bulb pattern** from page 150, and transfer it to the center of the rectangle using the carbon paper. Cut a 24-inch length of embroidery thread, and separate out a single strand to use. Embroider the lightbulb motif using a chain stitch (see page 149).

• **Fold the rectangle in half, right sides together.** Stitch the ends together.

• **Lay the double-sided tape** along the edges. Fold the top of the fabric over the top circle of the lampshade (the one that has a hole for inserting the light socket). Make small slits $^5/_8$-inch from the metal rods leading to the center of the frame. Remove the protection from the double-sided tape and attach [fig. 1]. Do the same on the bottom circle of the lampshade. Hang from your existing fixture.

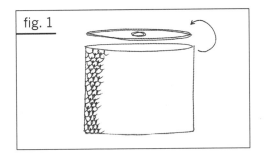

fig. 1

GLASS JARS

Don't hesitate to repurpose all sorts of jars to make these creations, such as those from jams, pickles, or preserves. You can also buy pretty mason jars new, or browse for cool old jars at flea markets and thrift stores or online.

INDUSTRIAL-CHIC JAR LAMP

A lamp in a jar, to stand or hang in any corner of your home.

TOOLS

drill
large and
small bits
round file
utility knife
small
screwdriver

SUPPLIES

1 medium-size
mason-type jar
1 brass
socket and
assorted $1/2$-
inch threaded
bushings
5-foot fabric-
covered electric
cord
1 black plug
1 light bulb

INSTRUCTIONS

• **Drill a hole** in the center of the jar's lid. File it down as needed so that your brass socket will fit. Then make 6 holes in the lid with a very small drill bit to keep the light bulb from overheating.

• **Strip $3/8$ inch of the cord** at one end with the utilty knife. Take two of the electric wires, and connect them to the socket using the small screwdriver.

• **Insert the socket** into the jar and pass the cord through the hole in the lid. Screw the bushing tightly into the lid. Strip the other end of the cord and connect to the electrical plug.

• **Screw in the light bulb** and close the jar.

HANGING CANDLE JAR

To add light to your garden or home.

TOOLS

cutting pliers
drill
small bit
medium brush

SUPPLIES

1 small jar
1 votive candle
1 old board
(from a pallet,
for example)
thin wire, 5 ft
1 small
screw-eye
S-hook
black paint
masking tape
1 paper tag
alphabet stamps
black ink

INSTRUCTIONS

• **Place masking tape** on the prettiest side of the board, 3/16 inch in from the outside edges to provide straight lines for painting a frame.

• **Paint the edges of** the board black, as well as the sides and top and bottom. Let dry.

• **Screw the screw-eye** into the center, 2 inches from the top of the board. Then drill a small hole, also in the center of the width, 3/4 inch from the top. This is for hanging the board on the wall.

• **Clean the jar**, completely removing labels and any glue left from them. Use Goo Gone or a similar cleaner if needed.

• **Cut 20 inches of the wire,** and fold it in half. Wrap it around the top of the jar, and twist tightly to form a snug ring around the opening. Next, cut a yard of wire and fold it in half to double it. Insert one end under the ring, and wind it several times around the ring. Do the same with the other end of the wire, on the side opposite to where you attached the first end. This is your hanging jar.

• **Place the hanging jar** on the S-hook, then hang the S hook on the screw-eye of the board.

• **Add a paper tag for a touch of whimsy,** and use black ink to stamp your message onto it.

ENMESHED HANGING VASES

Because macramé is trendy, and there's a desire for floating bouquets!

TOOLS	SUPPLIES	INSTRUCTIONS
scissors	1 medium-sized mason-type jar 1 roll of fairly thin natural twine	

INSTRUCTIONS

• **Note:** The instructions for making this craft are illustrated on page 151–152.

• **Cut eight 10-foot pieces** of twine. Fold them in half, to make sixteen 5-foot strands.

• **Take one of your pieces of twine,** and use it to bind the rest together, starting 1 3/16 inches before the center of the bunch, where they're folded. Keep circling the strand around for 2 3/8 inches.

• **Tie a simple knot** to close the final loop [fig. 2]. Now, hang it (over a chair, for example) in order to make the macramé weaving easier.

• **Divide the strands** into four groups of four strands each. Tie each group of four into a single knot, 11 3/4 inches from the knot on top [fig. 3, page 152]. Then, divide each of these sections in two at 3 1/2 inches below, and tie knots using the two strands from two adjacent sets [fig. 4]. Tie four knots like this, all the way around, to finish the pattern.

• **Repeat this series of knots** 2 inches lower, changing the strands as shown [fig. 5]. Tie a third series of knots 2 inches from the bottom in the same way. Finally, 2 inches below this last one, tie all the strands together in a simple knot [fig. 6].

• **Place the jar** in the center of the macramé holder.

STAMPED-LEATHER WINTER GARDEN

Stamped leather straps give your indoor garden a steampunk edge.

TOOLS

hammer
leathercraft
roller
leathercraft awl
or punch
needle

SUPPLIES

5 jars of
mixed sizes
1 20 x 20-inch
piece of natural
leather*
number stamps
for leather
leather
fertilized potting
soil
assorted small
plants (such as
succulents or
cacti)

INSTRUCTIONS

• **Cut leather strips of various widths** for the jars. To figure out how long to make them, measure the circumference of your jar and add $3/4$ inch.

• **Stamp the numbers** onto the straps using a hammer and the leather stamps.

• **Use a leather roller** to fold back $3/16$ inch from each end of the strap (see photo on page 73). Punch a hole through both thicknesses, and sew with a saddle stitch (see instructions on page 149).

• **Fill your jars** with soil, and plant your favorite plants. Slip on the leather bands.

* You can easily find pieces of leather and the necessary supplies in craft stories or online. (The leather shown here is sheepskin.)

TREASURES UNDER GLASS

Protect small souvenirs in a mason jar by creating a scene of pretty things.

TOOLS

medium, round
sash brush

SUPPLIES

1 large mason-
type jar
1 paper tag
alphabet stamps
black ink
floral foam
fabric flowers
and other small
treasures
off-white, matte
paint
masking tape

INSTRUCTIONS

• **Wrap the masking tape** around the jar 2 $^3/_8$ inches from the bottom to form a straight line for painting. Paint an off-white band on the bottom (below the tape), and let dry. Don't be too precise—the roughness is part of the charm.

• **Place** the floral foam (found in arts and crafts stores) in the bottom of the jar. Then stage your fabric flowers, as well as any other little treasures that you love, in the jar.

• **Stamp** "*happy*" on the tag in black ink, and attach it to a stem. Close the jar.

STRING OF LIGHTS

This softly-glowing string of lights is perfect for the corner of a shelf, on a party table, or on the ground.

TOOLS

sash brush
small cutting pliers
scissors
craft knife

SUPPLIES

20 small baby food jars
20 feet of 3 1/8-inch-wide plaster bandages
off-white paint
string of lights of 20 bulbs
fine wire

INSTRUCTIONS

• **Cut forty 3 1/8 x 3 1/8-inch squares** from the plaster bandage. Double them up, and cut the corners to make little circles.

• **Moisten your fingers with water,** and place one of the doubled circles over the jar's opening. Fold the edges, and stretch it tight over the jar's top, shaping it with your fingers while trying to fray the edges a bit. Let it dry and rinse off any plaster that has dripped down the sides of the jar. Repeat for the remaining jars.

• **Cut twenty 7 7/8-inch pieces** of wire. Wrap each piece of wire around the plaster near the top of the jar and twist the wire to tighten it.

• **Clean the jars** with a soft cloth. Once the plaster has totally dried, use a craft knife to cut a notch in the shape of a cross by making 2 3/8-inch slits in the center of the lid.

• **Turn the jars over,** and paint the bottoms off-white with a large, rough brush stroke. Let dry.

• **Insert one bulb** of the string of lights into each of the jars.

TRIO OF VASES

A few light flowers in a series of floating vases.

TOOLS

screwdriver
saw
drill
1-inch–diameter drillbit
small bit
number 2 pencil
ruler
scissors
superglue

SUPPLIES

1 board from a pallet
3 tall baby food jars
medium and fine grade sandpaper
6 small screws
cotton string

INSTRUCTIONS

• **Saw a board** (from a pallet or elsewhere) that's around 3 1/8 inches wide and 9 1/2 inches long. Sand the outside edges with medium-grade sand paper to get rid of splinters. Finish with fine sandpaper to make the wood nice and smooth.

• **Clean the jars,** completely removing labels and any glue left from them. Use Goo Gone or similar cleaner if needed.

• **Center the three lids** under the board, and screw them in with two small screws each. Place the screws as close to the edge of the lid as possible without making it difficult to close the jar.

• **Drill a hole** using the 1-inch diameter bit in the center of each lid, drilling all the way through the board. Sand the edges of the holes to get rid of splinters.

• **Mark four dots** with the pencil, two at each end of the board, 3/8 inch from the edge of the length, and 3/4 inch from the edge of the width.

• **Drill four small holes** using the small bit [fig. 1].

• **Cut two pieces** of cotton string, each 5 feet long. Thread the string through the holes, and tie a knot as in the drawing [fig. 2]. Slide the knot down close to the board. Trim the loose end of the string, and put a dot of superglue on the knot. Do the same thing on the other side.

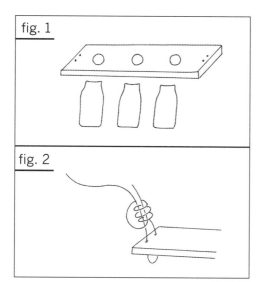

fig. 1

fig. 2

WINE
BOTTLES

Save wine bottles, all of them! They come in different colors (green, yellow, or clear) and somewhat varied shapes. You can also find old bottles in thrift shops. They're often quite beautiful ones with thick glass and rounded bases.

JOINED VASES

Take apart a bouquet, and arrange the flowers in an series of vases.

TOOLS

large mixing bowl
matches
1 1/8-inch crochet hook

SUPPLIES

6 to 10 glass bottles of varied shapes and colors*

rubbing alcohol

yarn or thick twine (100% natural)

coarse-grade sandpaper

gold cord

INSTRUCTIONS

• **Fill the large mixing bowl** with cold water and ice.

• **For each bottle, cut a piece of yarn** long enough to circle the bottle twice and to tie a double knot. Thoroughly wet the yarn in the alcohol and wrap the bottle twice at the point where you want it cut (straight across or diagonally). Tighten and double knot the yarn. Trim the ends of the yarn close to the knot.

• **Dry the bottle well**, and rinse your hands. Firmly hold the bottle horizontally, and light the yarn on fire. Let it burn while rotating the bottle. When the flame goes out, dip the bottle in the cold water. The bottle will be cleanly cut where the yarn was. If it doesn't turn out as you hoped, don't despair; just do it again!

• **Sand the bottle** to smooth any sharp edges.

• **Repeat this process** for the other five bottles, varying the height and angle at which you cut them [fig. 1].

• **Now make the chain** to tie the vases together. Crochet the gold thread to get a 6 1/2-foot-long chain (see page 148). Weave it around the bottles, and finish with a bow [fig. 2].

* You only need six bottles for this project, but it's good to have more on hand in case any of the bottles break.

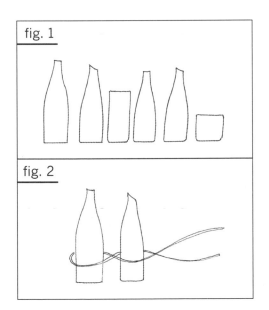

fig. 1

fig. 2

BULB STARTER

Force a bulb to grow without soil.

TOOLS

large mixing bowl
matches

SUPPLIES

1 to 2 clear glass bottles*
alcohol
yarn or thick twine (100% natural)
coarse-grade sandpaper
flower bulbs (such as hyacinth or amaryllis)
alphabet stamps
black ink

INSTRUCTIONS

• **Peel the labels off of the bottles** somewhat roughly to leave a thin layer of paper. Print whatever message you like in black ink on the remaining paper, using the stamps.

• **Cut the neck of the bottle** where it starts to widen, using the method explained on page 85. The sweet spot allows you to place the cut-off top of the bottle upside-down inside its base.

• **Sand the edges well,** and then place the top piece upside-down inside the base.

• **Fill the bottom with water,** and insert the bulb into the bottleneck.

• **Keep the container in a room** with bright, indirect light and watch the roots form. Add water as necessary to keep the level just where the root zone is forming. Over time you will see leaves and stems.

*Get more bottles than needed in case any bottles break.

to grow up

LUMINESCENT CANDLE JARS

Create a soft light and a cozy atmosphere with these candle jars.

TOOLS

large mixing bowl

matches

SUPPLIES

3 to 5 glass bottles*

alcohol

yarn or thick twine (100% natural)

coarse grain sandpaper

tealight candles

INSTRUCTIONS

- **Cut the bottles** using the method described on page 85.

- **Sand the edges.**

- **Place the bottle tops** over lit tealight candles.

*You only need three bottles for this project, but you should have more in case any break during the cutting.

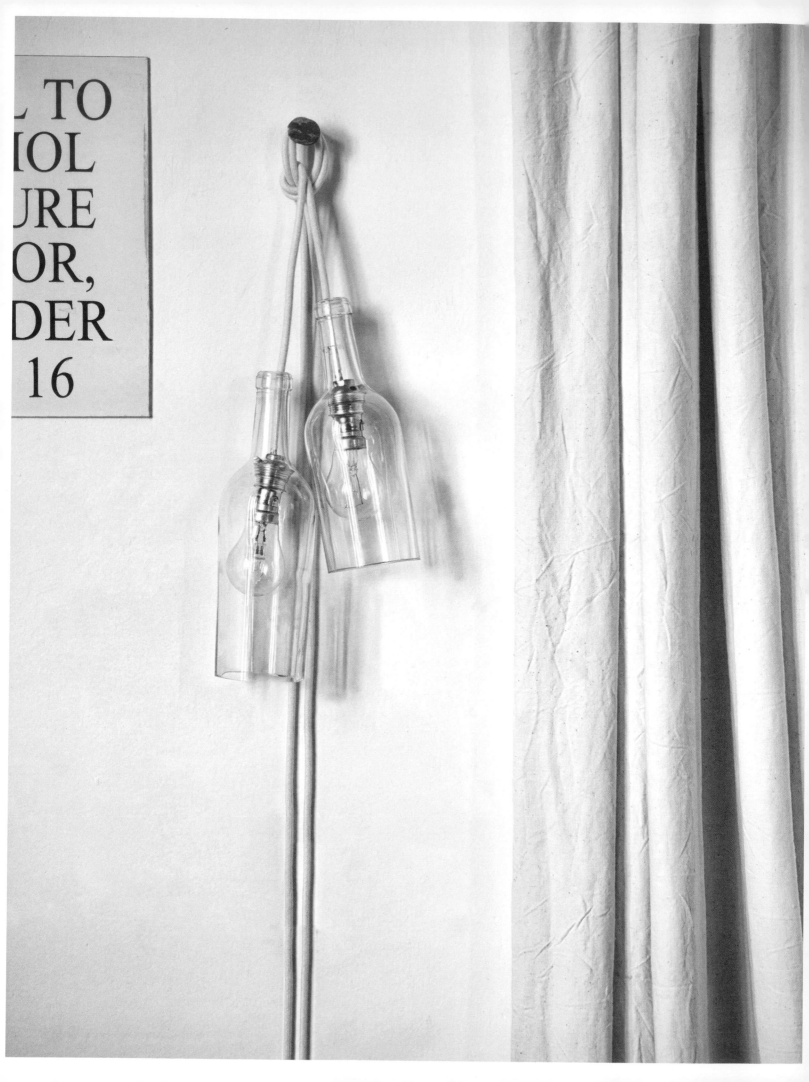

HANGING LAMPS

Made from clear or colored glass, these lamps brighten up any room.

TOOLS

large mixing bowl
matches
1 small screwdriver for electric wires

SUPPLIES

2 to 3 clear glass bottles*
alcohol
yarn or thick twine (100% natural)
coarse grain sandpaper
2 "make-a-lamp" kits
2 light bulbs

INSTRUCTIONS

• **Cut the bottoms off the bottles** using the method described on page 85.

• **Sand the edges carefully.**

• **Follow the manufacturer's instructions** to assemble simple pendant lamps from a kit. Pass the cord through the bottle, and join it to the socket [fig. 1]. If you're comfortable working with electricity, you can do the entire setup yourself using cotton-wrapped electrical cord and brass sockets to customize your look.

• **Screw the light bulbs** into each of the sockets.

• **Hang the lamps from ceiling fixtures,** or knot the cord to create a wall lamp that hangs from a nail [fig. 2].

* You only need two bottles for this project, but have more in case of breakage during the cutting.

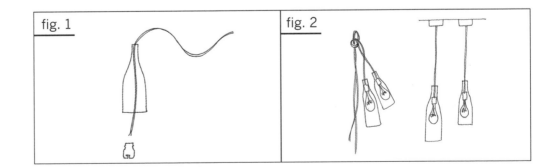

fig. 1

fig. 2

VASE DRESSED IN A SWEATER

A single flower or a pretty branch is enough to decorate this wintry vase.

TOOLS

1 pair of n° 4
knitting needles
1 large-eye
needle

SUPPLIES

1 glass bottle
1 natural-color
ball of wool

INSTRUCTIONS

• **Cast on 20 stitches,** and then knit 17 rows using stockinette stitches.

• **Every four stitches,** add one stitch—that is, four additions per row (but not adding a stitch after the last four stitches of the row)—starting from the 18th row. Repeat for a total of eight rows. You'll then have 52 stitches in the eighth row.

• **Continue** to knit 20 rows of stockinette stitches after the 25th row.

• **Cast off your stitches,** and finish by joining the two parts of your "sweater" by stitching on the underside [fig. 1].

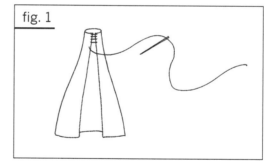

fig. 1

A BOTTLE OF LIGHT

For a cozy atmosphere, think about putting a simple string of lights under glass!

TOOLS	SUPPLIES	INSTRUCTIONS
large mixing bowl matches	1 to 2 glass bottles (with cork)* alcohol yarn or thick twine (100% natural) coarse-grade sandpaper 1 file 1 small string of lights	• **Cut off the bottoms of the bottles** using the method described on page 85. • **Sand the edges** carefully. • **File a small notch** into the bottom edge for the lights' cord. • **Place the string of lights** in the bottle, plug it in, and turn on the lights.

* Get more bottles than needed in case any break while cutting.

TIN CANS

Take a tin can, remove the label, and you have the base for any number of projects . . . Cans come in a range of sizes—make use of them all!

KNITTED-TWINE PLANTERS

Dress tin cans in twine to make fun and funky planters.

TOOLS

1 pair of n° 10 (or n° 6 if using thinner twine) knitting needles
1 large-eye needle
tape measure

SUPPLIES

1 medium tin can
1 ball of natural twine, fine or medium
fertilized potting soil
small plant (such as a succulent, cactus, or wheatgrass)

INSTRUCTIONS

• **Wash and dry** the can. Remove the label and, if necessary, use Goo Gone or similar cleaner to remove any traces of glue.

• **Begin knitting by casting on 10 stitches** in four rows. Remove the needles, and measure the length you knitted. Then measure the circumference of your can.

• **Figure out the number of stitches** that you'll need for this project—so, if your test row of 10 stitches measures 2 inches and you want to make 4 inches total, you'll need 20 stitches, and so forth.

• **Once you've figured out** the number of stitches you'll need according to your can's circumference, knit about 15 rows (depending on your can's height) using garter stitches. Bind off.

• **Sew the two short sides** of the rectangle together using the large-eye needle and one strand of the twine.

• **Slide the knitted cover onto your can,** and add potting soil and the plant of your choice.

A CROSS-STITCHED CANDLE

Light and texture come together with a simple message.

TOOLS

1 needle
1 double boiler
double-sided tape

SUPPLIES

1 medium can (3 3/8-inch diameter)
1 12 x 5 1/4-inch piece of cardboard
spray adhesive
white linen for cross stitching
1 skein of black cotton embroidery thread
wax pellets
1 cotton wick
1 wood skewer
aluminum foil

INSTRUCTIONS

• **Cut a 12 x 6-inch rectangle** from the linen. Mark the center, and lay your rectangle in front of you lengthwise. Cut a 24-inch piece of thread, and separate out a single strand. Thread the needle, double the thread, and knot.

• **Cross-stitch the message** using the pattern on page 153. Wash and dry the embroidered linen—don't iron it; you want it to stay lightly wrinkled.

• **Lay the embroidered fabric** wrong side up. Next, spray your cardboard with the adhesive, and place it on the fabric, centered vertically, which allows for 3/8-inch hems on top and bottom. Fold the hems over the cardboard, and fasten with double-sided tape.

• **Place another layer of double-sided tape** on the hemmed edges, and wrap your embroidered linen around the can. Tape the short ends together to finish.

• **Melt the wax in a double boiler.** Then, cut a 7-inch piece of wick. Once the wax begins to melt, dip the wick into it to coat it thoroughly. Remove the wick, and lay it on a piece of aluminum foil. Roll the foil carefully to keep the wick straight, then put it in the freezer for at least five minutes.

• **Wind one end of the hardened wick** around the middle of the skewer. Hold the skewer above the can, so that the wick is at the center. Make sure it's long enough to touch the bottom.

• **Holding the wick centered,** pour the melted wax into the can up to about 3/16 inch from the top edge.

• **Put the candle in the fridge** for about three hours. Holes might form at the surface of the candle as it dries. If this happens, melt a little more wax, and pour it on top.

• **Cut the wick** to about 3/4 inch.

DESK ORGANIZER

Keep those pens and pencils organized.

TOOLS

number 2
pencil
needle

SUPPLIES

5 cans
(3 medium
and 2 large)
1 yard of
$5/8$-inch wide
ecru grosgrain
ribbon
1 skein of
black cotton
embroidery
thread
black spray
paint
tracing paper
carbon paper
superglue

INSTRUCTIONS

• **Spray-paint the interiors and exteriors** of the cans black. Let them dry according to the manufacturer's instructions. Add a second coat, and let it dry again.

• **Trace the pattern** "organise it" (page 153), and transfer it to the grosgrain ribbon using carbon paper and pencil.

• **Embroider the message** using a chain stitch (see page 149) and one strand of the black embroidery thread.

• **Stack the cans on their sides** like a pyramid (three on the bottom and two on the top), and hold them together with the embroidered ribbon. Tighten the ribbon, and glue its ends together underneath the cans.

organise it !

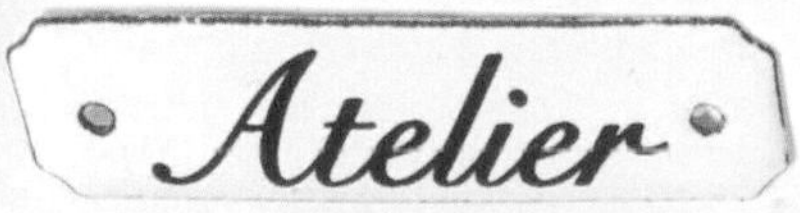
Atelier

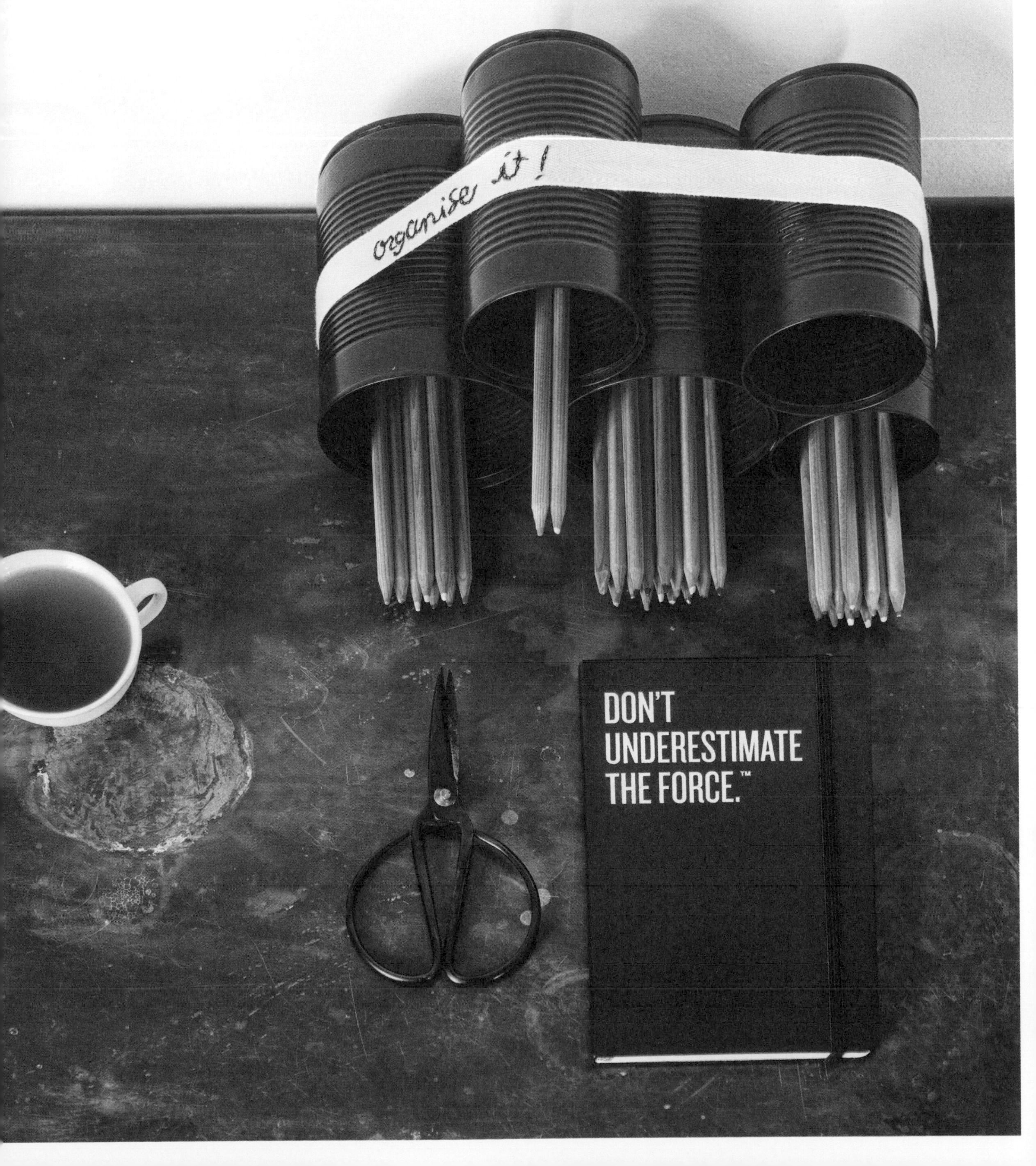
organise it!
DON'T UNDERESTIMATE THE FORCE.™

HANGING CUTLERY TINS

To separate spoons from forks, and maybe you can add a pretty succulent . . .

TOOLS	SUPPLIES	INSTRUCTIONS

TOOLS

hammer
label maker

SUPPLIES

3 medium cans
3 yards of ecru cotton string
nail
spray paint (matte ecru)
super glue

INSTRUCTIONS

• **Gently tap the cans** with a hammer in order to lightly dent them.

• **Spray-paint the cans inside and out** with the ecru paint. Let them dry according to the manufacturer's instructions, then add a second coat and let dry again..

• **Punch two holes** across from each other in the top edge of each can, $3/8$ inch from the top edge, by tapping the nail through from the inside of the can.

• **Cut the cotton cord** into three 1-yard pieces. Thread the cord through each hole, and tie a knot on each end as shown [fig. 1]. Tighten each knot, trim the loose end, and then tighten the knot at the edge of the can. Trim the cord next to the knot, and add a dot of glue. Repeat the process for the two remaining cans.

• **Make three labels**—"(UN)", "(DEUX)", and "(TROIS)"— using the label maker, and stick them onto the cans.

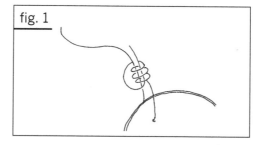

fig. 1

FESTIVE BELLS

DIY bells add a touch of whimsy to any room.

TOOLS

medium brush
hammer

SUPPLIES

3 small tin cans
6 ½ yards of
5-inch-wide
plaster bandage
all-purpose paint
(ecru matte)
natural twine
3 wooden beads
nail

INSTRUCTIONS

• **For each bell**, pierce a hole in the bottom of the can using the hammer and nail.

• **Paint the inside of the cans** with the ecru paint, and then let it dry. Add a second coat and let it dry again.

• **Tie a double knot** at the end of a 1 ½-yard piece of twine. String a wooden bead onto the twine. Then thread the twine through the hole in the can (starting from the exterior), and tie another double knot 2 ³/₈ inches from the edge [fig. 1]. Repeat the process for each can.

• **Moisten the plaster with warm water,** and wrap it twice around each can, smoothing it on with your fingers.

• **Pull gently** on the bottom of the fabric to fray it, and then let it dry.

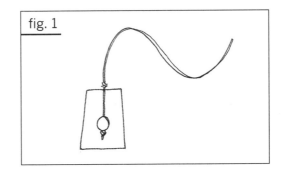

fig. 1

LAMPSHADES

Repurpose lampshade frames, or buy them in arts and crafts stores. Revitalize old lamps by using them to beautify a space.

RE-COVERED SHADE

Add a knitted lampshade to a frame and create a rustic chic decoration.

TOOLS

1 large-eye
needle
1 pair of n° 10
knitting needles

SUPPLIES

1 spool of
medium natural
twine

1 11 ¾ inch
diameter
hanging
lampshade
frame

1 black hanging-
lamp light cord
with socket and
lightbulb

INSTRUCTIONS

• **Knit** 48 stitches with the natural twine. Knit 13 rows of garter stitches, keeping them fairly loose. Finish by binding off.

• **Thread the needle** with one strand of the twine and sew a seam joining the two short ends.

• **Attach the knitted cover** to the lampshade. Stitch the upper edge of the knitting to the upper circle of the lampshade [fig. 1].

• **Attach the socket** to the lampshade, by screwing it into the electric cord, and then screw in a lightbulb.

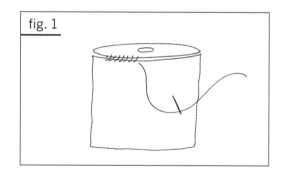

fig. 1

DREAM CATCHER

Make meditative art for your bedroom.

TOOLS

scissors

SUPPLIES

1 round lampshade frame, 9 7/8-inch diameter
2 skeins of matte twisted cotton yarn for tapestry (gray and green)
feathers and assorted beads
superglue

• **Cut one yard** of the green thread.

• **Tie one end in a knot** around the metal circle [fig. 1], and then keep knotting the thread, going all the way around the circle until it's completely wrapped [fig. 2]. Tighten it as you go. Then put a dot of glue on the end of the strand before tying your final knot.

• **Using a new piece of yarn**, tie a secure knot every 1 1/2 inches counterclockwise around your circle, making loops as in the drawing [fig. 3]. On the second time around, tie the knots in the centers of the preceding loops [fig. 4]. Continue like this until you reach the center [fig. 5]. Pull the yarn to pull it toward the center as in the drawing [fig. 6], and finish by tying a triple knot.

• **Fold two 10-inch strands of gray yarn** in half, and knot them below the circle [fig. 7]. Thread beads on each strand, and attach them with a simple knot. Finish by tying on a feather.

• **Knot one end of the thread** 11 3/4 inches from the top of the circle so that you can hang your dream catcher.

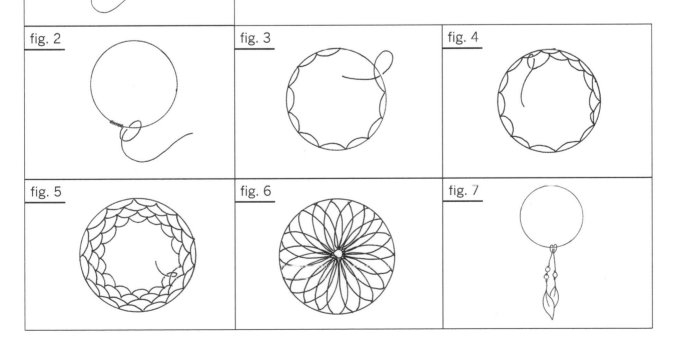

fig. 1

fig. 2

fig. 3

fig. 4

fig. 5

fig. 6

fig. 7

WHIMSICAL WALL HANGINGS

Add a unexpected pop of color to a dull corner.

TOOLS

scissors
1/8-inch
crochet needle

SUPPLIES

1 bell-shaped
lampshade
frame
1 metal
lampshade
hanger
5 or 6 balls of
wool in assorted
colors
superglue

INSTRUCTIONS

• **Cut several 1-yard** pieces of wool.

• **Wrap the metal hangers with one color of wool** by tying knots all the way down each one. Tighten as you go. To finish, put a dot of glue on the end of the strand before tying the final knot.

• **Crochet one yard of wool** of any color using a chain stitch (see page 148).

• **Cross two strands** of yarn at the center of the lampshades' upper circle. Then knot your chain at the intersection of the two strands. Make several of these little decorative shades and hang anywhere you want to add color to a room.

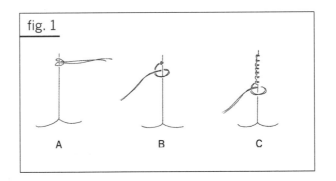

fig. 1

A   B   C

AFFIRMATION MOBILE

Remind yourself to stay positive with this breezy mobile.

TOOLS

utility knife
ruler
needle

SUPPLIES

1 lampshade frame circle, 10-inch diameter
white drawing paper
alphabet stamps
black ink
transparent nylon string
white cotton thread
superglue

INSTRUCTIONS

• **Use the utility knive to cut** the paper into rectangles of varying sizes: 4 ³/₄ x 4 ³/₄ inches, 5 x 3 ¹/₂ inches, and 4 x 2 ³/₄ inches.

• **Stamp some messages** in black ink on your paper rectangles. Here, I chose a mix of French and English phrases that birghten my day or make me smile.

• **Cut strands** of white cotton string (between 8 and 12 inches), and then use the need to thread them through the paper rectangles' top, center edge. Tie knots and let the loose strands hang.

• **Knot together** four pieces of the transparent nylon thread, each one yard long. Next, knot the ends of each thread at the four quarters of the lampshade circle. Secure the knots with a dot of glue. You can now hang your mobile. Finish by tying your messages all the way around the circle.

DISHWARE

Hunt for pleasing, white dishes at flea markets, garage sales, thrift stores, or on eBay; you can repurpose plates of all sizes, cups and saucers, and more. It's also surprisingly affordable to buy new porcelain pieces at a discount store or online.

HAND-PAINTED WALL DECOR

Move the porcelain maker's mark from the back to the front for a quirky, random display.

TOOLS

number 2 pencil

SUPPLIES

6 white plates
(3 small
and 3 large)
carbon paper
tracing paper
porcelain felt
pens (peacock
blue and black)
6 picture-
hanging
adhesive strips

INSTRUCTIONS

• **Wash and dry** the plates.

• **Trace the designs** (pages 154 to 156) using tracing paper, and then transfer them onto the plates using carbon paper.

• **Draw the designs** with the porcelain felt pen. Let dry and place the plates in the oven, following the manufacturer's directions to set the ink.

• **Place adhesive strips** on the back of each plate, top center, to hang them.

*since
1775.*

CUP AND CREAMER CANDLES

Mix-and-match white porcelain vessels for an adorable arrangement of candles.

TOOLS

double boiler
heat resistant
bowl

SUPPLIES

cups and
creamers
wax pellets
1 cotton wick
wooden skewers
aluminum foil

INSTRUCTIONS

• **Wash and dry** the cups and creamers.

• **Melt the wax** in a double boiler. Cut pieces of wick that are equal to the depth of your containers plus 1 $1/2$ inches. For each candle, once the wax begins to melt, stick the wick into it to coat it thoroughly, and then remove it. Lay the wick on a piece of aluminum foil, and roll it in the foil to keep it straight. Put it in the freezer for at least five minutes.

• **Wind one end** of the hardened wick around the middle of the skewer. Then place each skewer on the edges of your containers, so that the wick touches the bottom. Make sure it's well centered for when you pour in the wax.

• **Pour the melted wax** into the cup or creamer up to about $3/16$ inch from the rim. Be sure the wick stays properly centered.

• **Put the candle in the fridge** for around three hours. Holes might form at the surface of the candle as it dries. If this happens, melt a little more wax, and pour it on top.

• **Cut the wick** to $5/8$ inch above the candle.

BACKDROP OF BROKEN TILES

A spontaneously-tiled mosaic for a pale, monochrome background.

TOOLS

hammer
sponge
small roller
plastic spatula

SUPPLIES

3 to 4 white plates
1 9 $^7/_8$- x 13 $^3/_4$-inch wood board
glue for tiles
plaster
1 sturdy plastic bag
off-white, matte paint

INSTRUCTIONS

• **Break the plates** one-by-one. To do this, put the plate in the plastic bag, and hit it with a hammer just enough to get small pieces of porcelain. Repeat for all the plates. Then pick the prettiest pieces, taking care not to cut yourself!

• **Using the spatula**, spread the glue about $^1/_8$-inch thick on a quarter of the board's surface (not more at a time because the glue dries quickly).

• **Position pieces of the broken porcelain.** Start at the edge of the board, and space your pieces with $^1/_{16}$- to $^3/_{16}$-inch gaps between them. Make sure to align them evenly with the edges of the board. Continue like this until the board is entirely covered. Let dry for around two hours (or as directed by the instructions on your glue container).

• **Prepare the plaster** by mixing the powder and water. The consistency should be similar to toothpaste. You now have to move fast because the plaster hardens very quickly. Pour the plaster over the porcelain pieces, filling the gaps and smoothing the surface with the spatula. Make sure all the gaps are filled.

• **Moisten the sponge,** and then wring it out out. Wipe the plaster off the tiles and remove any extra plaster. Repeat the process several times until your mosaic is perfectly clean.

• **Let the mosaic dry**, then clean the sides of the board with the sponge. Let it dry, and then add three coats of paint on the sides with the roller, being careful not to get any paint on the mosaic.

CLOCK ON A PLATE

It's always the right time with this charming clock on your wall.

TOOLS

auger bit
drill
clamp
number 2 pencil

SUPPLIES

1 white plate
1 clock
mechanism
with hands
carbon paper
tracing paper
1 porcelain felt
pen (black)
1 picture
hanging
adhesive strip

INSTRUCTIONS

• **Wash and dry** the plate.

• **Use the auger bit** to drill a hole in the plate's center. It's important to hold the plate steady (by clamping it to a wood block for example). You can also have someone hold the plate in place while you drill.

• **Trace the design** (page 157) using tracing paper, and transfer it onto the plate using carbon paper.

• **Color the designs** with the porcelain felt pen. Let dry, and then place the plate in the oven following the manufacturer's directions to set the ink.

• **Attach the clock mechanism,** being sure to screw the bolt tightly. Set the hands to the correct time.

• **Place the adhesive strip** on the back, top-center of the clock mechanism behind the plate in order to hang the clock. (Some mechanisms also have a built-in hanging point if you prefer to use that.)

STACKED CANDLE-HOLDER

Perch a candle atop a sturdy stack of cups.

TOOLS

SUPPLIES

4 white porcelain cups and saucers in a variety of shapes and sizes

superglue

candle

INSTRUCTIONS

• **Wash and dry** the cups and saucers.

• **Stack the cups** and saucers from large to small. Put some cups upside down, and be sure to finish with the smallest cup on top, as that's where you'll put the candle.

• **Glue the cups** and saucers together.

• **Place the candle** Inside the smallest cup.

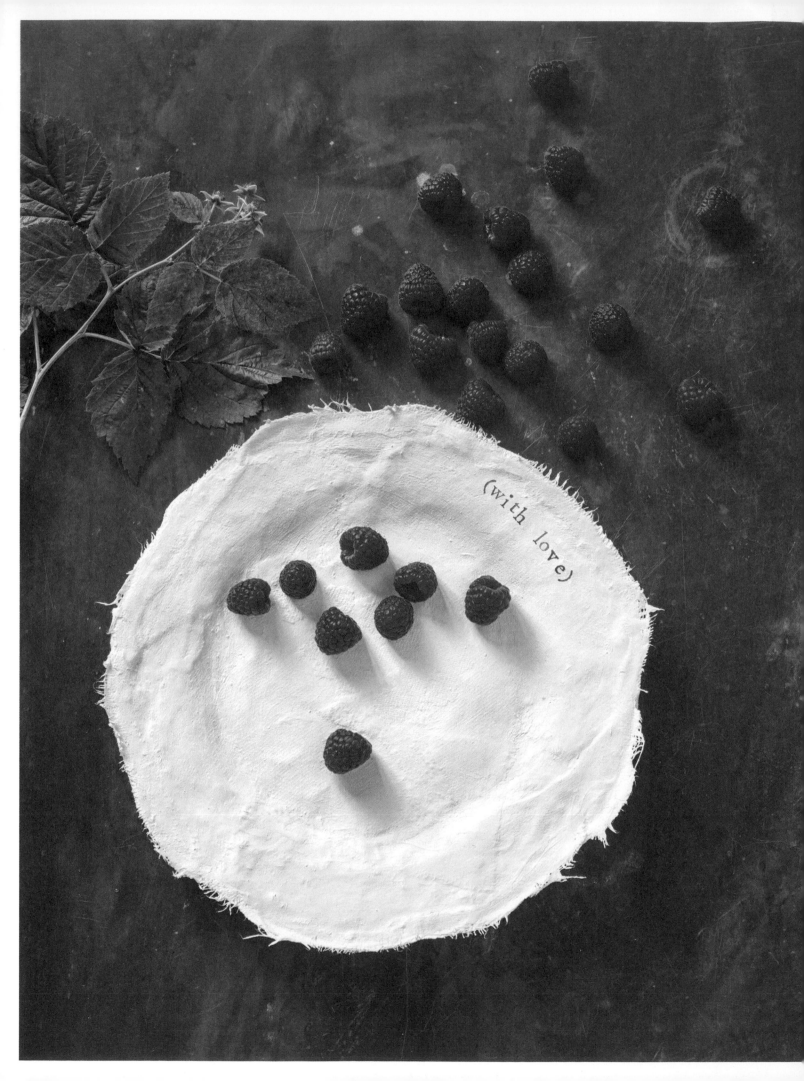

A DISH PLASTERED WITH LOVE

Design an artsy plate with frayed borders and lots of love.

TOOLS

alphabet stamps

SUPPLIES

1 white plate
20 feet of plaster bandage, 3 1/8-inch wide
black ink

INSTRUCTIONS

• **Wash and dry** the plate.

• **Wrap the plaster bandage** around the plate, covering it completely [fig. 1].

• **Moisten the plaster** with warm water to make it stick, and smooth it with your fingers. Repeat the process, this time wrapping it perpendicularly to the first layer. Repeat one last time, again perpendicularly to the preceding layer. Smooth each layer well as you go.

• **Cut the plaster bandages** into 7 7/8-inch strips, and cut those again in half lengthwise. Place these all around the rim of the plate, and then pull gently on the horizontal threads of the plaster to fray it [fig. 2]. Let dry two days.

• **Stamp** your message in black ink along the edge.

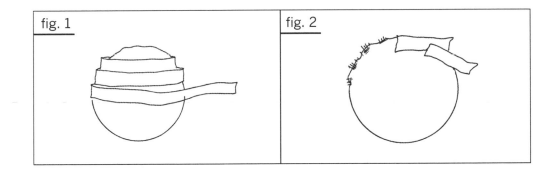

fig. 1

fig. 2

PATTERNS + MORE

The instructions in this section will help you create the projects in this book. The traceable designs and words you'll find here will inspire you to cut, stitch, embroider, paint, and draw a home-full of upcycled decor.

0123456789

(abcdefghijklm
nopqrstuvwxyz)

For the "stars" headboard (page 17)

STARS

For the fire-log holder (page 34)

FIRE

For the message boards (page 22)

Folie douce

{ it's time } ENJOY

Papillon

minute happiness

petit BOUDOIR

TRESORS rose

lundi

vendredi

samedi

dimanche

mardi

mercredi

jeudi

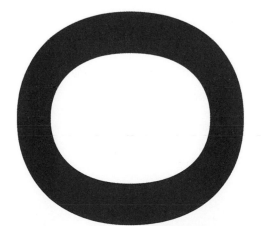

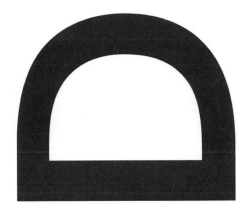

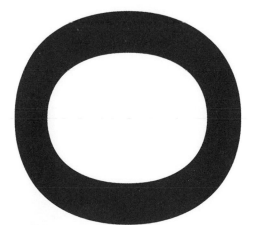
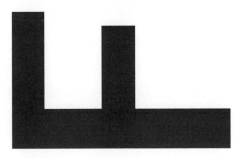

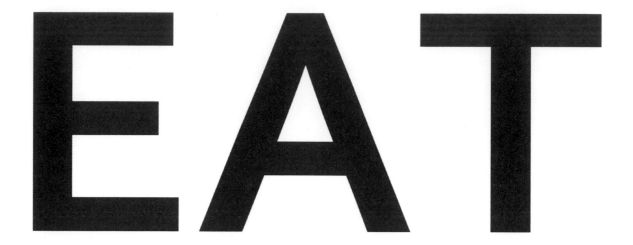

Crochet chain stitch

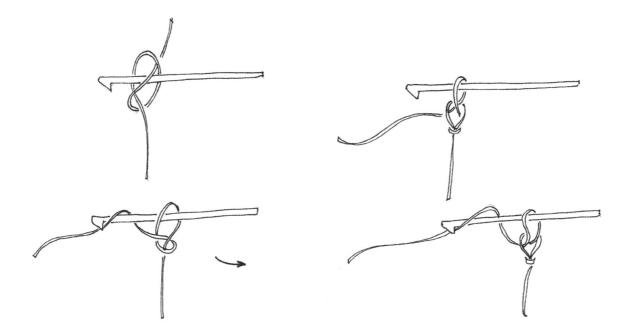

Blanket stitch

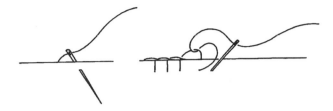

Saddle stitch

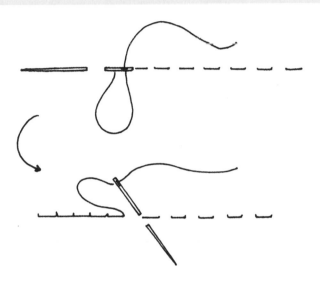

Chain stitch

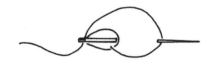

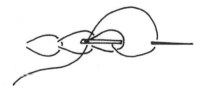

Put the light on

For the enmeshed hanging vases (page 71)

fig. 1

fig. 2

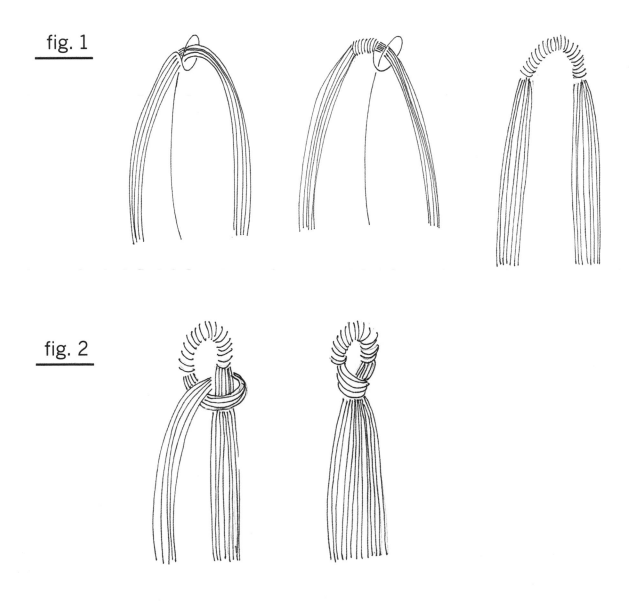

fig.3

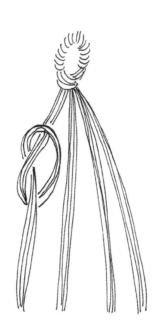

fig. 4

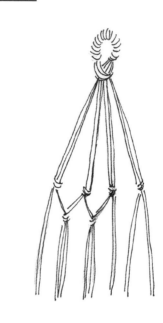

fig. 5

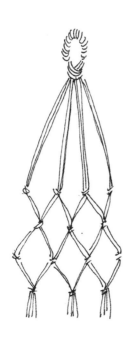

fig. 6

For the cross-stitched candle (page 103)

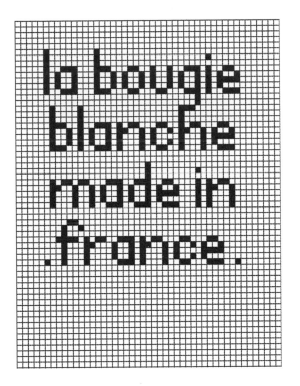

For the desk organizer (page 104)

organise it !

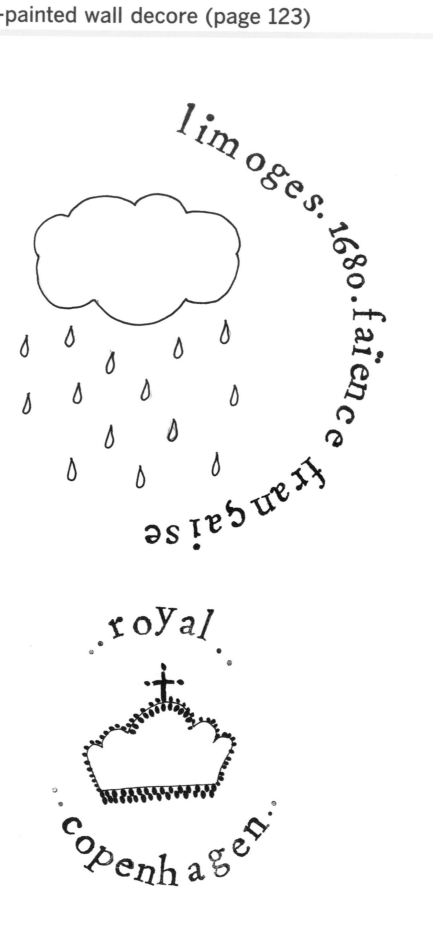

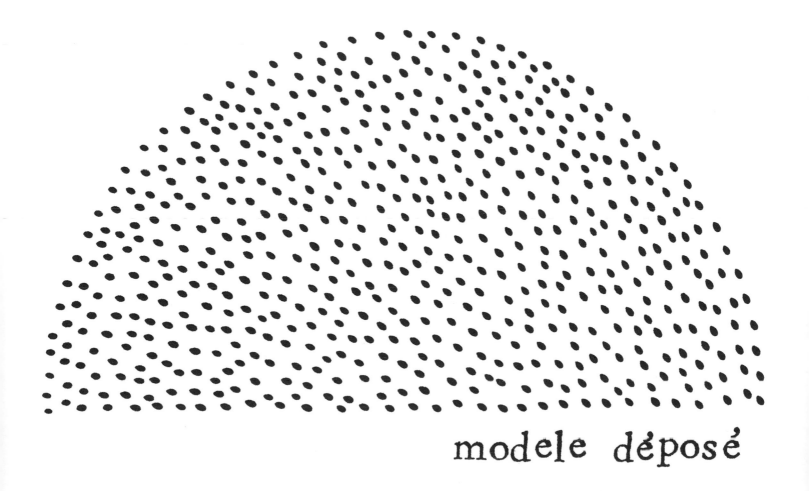

since
1775.

my

white

home

modele déposé

Middle of the plate

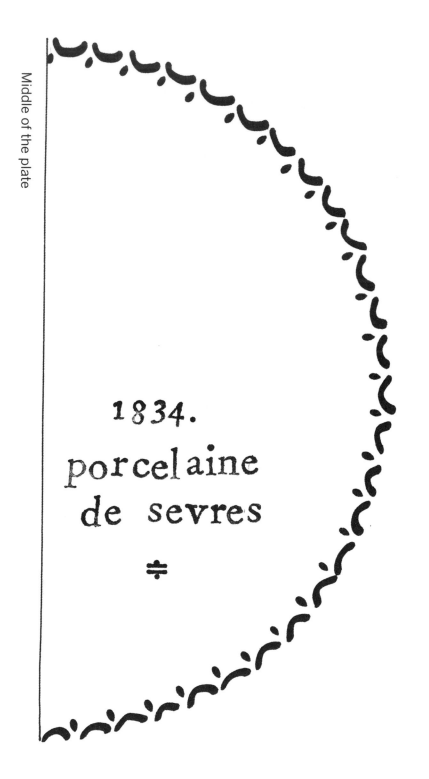

1834.

porcelaine
de sevres

÷

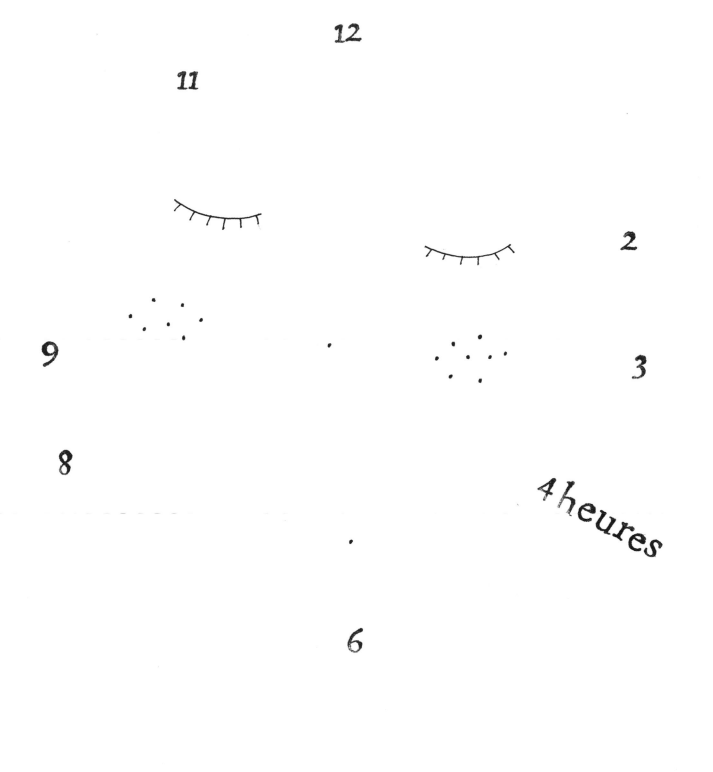

INDEX

From the author:

A big thank you to Farrow & Ball FARROW & BALL for the paints that were used in making all the projects in this book. www.farrow-ball.com

weldon**owen**

PRESIDENT & PUBLISHER Roger Shaw

SVP, SALES & MARKETING Amy Kaneko

ASSOCIATE PUBLISHER Mariah Bear

ASSOCIATE EDITOR Ian Cannon

CREATIVE DIRECTOR Kelly Booth

ART DIRECTOR Allister Fein

ASSOCIATE PRODUCTION DIRECTOR Michelle Duggan

IMAGING MANAGER Don Hill

ENGLISH TRANSLATION Sarah Levin

Weldon Owen would like to thank Brittany Bogan for proofreading the English edition.

Originally published in 2016 as Détournez les Objects du Quotidien

© Hachette Livre (Hachette Pratique)

Printed in China

ISBN 978-1-68188-367-0